MIMSISM's

Blow your horn.

85 LIFE PRACTICES FOR ACHIEVING SUCCESSES

Volume Two
2018

By Frank Mims V

Blow your horn.

Satya Nadella
CEO, Microsoft

"Companies like ours need to have a set of principles that really help us protect the enduring values and so do the people that we employ."

Blow your horn.

Copyright © 2018 Frank Mims V

All rights reserved. Except as permitted under the U. S. Copyright Act of 1976, no part of this publication may be reproduced, distributed, or transmitted in any form or by any means, or stored in a database, or retrieval system, without the prior written permission of the publisher.

Published in United State by Blow Your Horn March 24, 2018

MIMSISM'S: 85 LIFE PRACTICES FOR ACHIEVING SUCCESSES

ISBN: 978-1985733404

Printed in the United States of America

 Blow your horn.

SIMPLE RULES
TO WINNING THE
GAME OF LIFE

Blow your horn.

Directions, Leadership, Clarity, Understanding, and Moral Compass

Blow your horn.

To: The Victims of the 54 mass shooting in the United States since the first day of the year 2000.

Blow your horn.

Timeline | US school shootings in 2018 starting from January 1st and ending on February 14 Valentine Day 45 days into the new year.

.

St Johns, January 3
A 31-year-old man died from a self-inflicted gunshot wound at East Olive Elementary School in Michigan.

Seattle, January 4
A gunshot was fired at the New Start High School in Washington State. The bullet entered an office window. No one was hurt.

Sierra Vista, January 10
A teen was found dead from a self-inflicted gunshot wound in a bathroom at Coronado Elementary School in Arizona.

San Bernardino, January 10

Blow your horn.

At least one shot was fired, shattering a California State University classroom window. There were no injuries.

Denison, January 10
A bullet was accidentally fired through a classroom wall at the Grayson College Criminal Justice Centre in Texas. No one was hurt.

Marshall, January 15
A bullet went through a residential hall's dorm room at the Wiley College Campus in Texas. No injuries were reported.

Winston-Salem, January 20
A state university football player was shot and killed at an event at Wake Forest University.

Italy, January 22
A teenage girl was wounded at Italy High school in Texas after a 16-year-old suspect opened fire with a semi-automatic handgun.

Blow your horn.

Gentilly, January 22
A shooting outside The NET Charter High School in Louisiana injured a 14-year-old boy.

Benton, January 23
Two people were killed and another 15 were shot at Marshall County High School in Kansas.

Mobile, January 25
Student Jonah Neal fired a gun on campus at Murphy High School in Alabama. No one was injured.

Dearborn, January 26
Shots were fired from a car in Dearborn High School's car park in Michigan. No injuries were reported.

Philadelphia, January 31
Gunshots erupted as a fight broke out outside of Lincoln High School. A 32-year-old man was shot twice and later pronounced dead.

Blow your horn.

Los Angeles, February 1
The accidental shooting injured five children at the Salvador B. Castro Middle School.

Oxon Hill, February 5
A teen was shot outside of Oxon Hill High School in Maryland. The victim survived.

Maplewood, February 5
A third-grader pulled the trigger on an officer's gun, firing a shot at the Harmony Learning Centre in Minnesota. No one was hurt.

New York, February 8
A teenager was taken into custody after a shot was fired inside Metropolitan High School. No one was hurt.

Parkland, February 14
A 19-year-old gunman returned to a Florida high school where he had once been expelled for disciplinary reasons and opened fire with an

Blow your horn.

New Approaches

To develop pointed Directions in life, reverberating Leadership skills, Clarity, of course, Understanding the benefits of all that surrounds you and the benefits you will bring, and an apparent Moral Compass to shield you from all life's pitfalls you must have some comprehensible guidelines to follow. To obtain these five constituents listed above YOU must first set objectives and parameters to govern your day to day activities. Action toward those you see daily and those you don't know. Mimsism's are such actions that will guide and coach you to a safe and successful life journey.

Blow your horn.

Introduction

Success is defined simply as the accomplishment of one's goals. Goals are the result of achievement toward which effort and discipline are directed. "He has achieved the success that has lived well, laughed often, and loved much." For everyone that has goals and techniques to achieve them each will choose a different method based on their teachings and life's journey. So, how do we edify the rules and policies of accomplishing goals that lead to successes? The answer is straightforward you instruct on the set of

Blow your horn.

decrees that govern SUCCESS. This is what MIMSISMs were written to accomplish.

MIMSISMs are these sets of decrees. These are the citations that delineate the rules that govern real SUCCESS. To know these regulations makes the goals easy to accomplish. My name is Frank Mims V and MIMSISMs are named after the four Frank Mims that preceded me and my maternal grandfather Ervin E. Larvan. They are quotes and aphorism that gave me insight and a direction to achieve my goals in life. It was the rules that were passed down to me in hopes that they would channel me through the

Blow your horn.

landmines of life. This book seeks to pass on the dos and does of just how to become successful, contented, well balanced, and at peace in your day-to-day life.

Moving through life can be complicated and perplexing. It helps to know the regulations and the convention to align your thought with your actions. The best way to achieve the great result through the use of MIMSISMs is to read them all. Then choose your top five that you will call your own. These five rules/quotes become the direction for success in life. They open new doors because you see

Blow your horn.

things differently because of your new standards.

What is a MIMSISM?

Many times in business and one's personal life's it becomes a necessity to have that designer statement or groups of words that will convey and ignite that internal flame within. MIMSISMs are just those types of quotations, haiku's or spits. Give direction, quotations, haiku's or spits that provide understanding and quotations, haiku's or spits that encouragement with direction when going through a storm. MIMSISMs are short instructional sentences

Blow your horn.

that provide clarity and routes for achieving success and accomplishing goals.

There is a factual need to have direction and insight to grow and mature in this 21st century. MIMSISMs are your GPS, giving routing and commands to get you where you must go.

If you don't have the weaponry in your moral arsenal to combat the wickedness and that gives you the ethical backbone to withstand the barrage of non-ideas and mistrusts that seek to discontinue you in the pursuit of your life goals, then success will always elude you.

 Blow your horn.

Quotes with Definitions

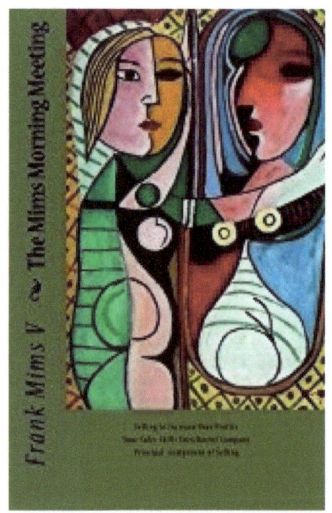

Blow your horn.

 Blow your horn.

Here are some comprehensive citations to govern activity and how to implement each one.

Blow your horn.

MIMSISM # 01 SEEK TO UNDERSTAND YOUR ENVIRONMENT, AND THEN IMPROVE IT.

Your environment is the earth worldwide. Don't limit yourself. Absolute comprehension of this one in a lifetime journal is demanded success. How do the pieces fit to become the sum of a hole?

MIMSISM # 02 BE ABLE TO ARTICULATE AND DEFEND YOUR VIEWPOINTS AND EXCEPT OTHERS.

Using the correct words and phrases to support, defend and convey your mindset is essences for success.

MIMSISM # 03 FIND THE REEL VEHICLES THAT WILL COERCE YOU TO YOUR DESTINATIONS WITH ACCOMPLISHMENT, METHOD, AND CLASS.

 Blow your horn.

No two vehicles will every look alike. Find YOUR, success is around the corner and up the hill.

MIMSISM # 04 DREAM OUTSIZED.

Let all your dreams be larger than you can envision. Just like Burger King has increase profits and sold more fries and soft drinks by super-sizing, you must super-size your dreams then make them happen, start now.

MIMSISM # 05 SEARCH FOR CHANGE-THEN CHANGE AGAIN.

Never become comfortable with your station in life. The ability to revolutionize your life's knowledge bank is growth and success.

MIMSISM # 06 MEET EVERY CHALLENGE WITH AN EDUCATED BATTLE.

Blow your horn.

Life must have challenges that move you out of your comfort zone. To fail is excellent. That uneasy sensation in the pit of your stomach is you growing. To overcome each challenge you will face staying well-read, overly informed and focus on the missions of success.

MIMSISM # 07 IF IT COST YOU NOTHING- IT IS WORTH NOTHING TO YOU AND TO ANYONE ELSE.

Your money, blood, sweat, ideas, and tears are all examples of value. Success is derived when you expend one, any or all of these to another.

MIMSISM # 08 BECOME A PROBLEM SEEKER, AND THEN BE A PROBLEM SOLVER.

Success will only be achieved and continued to be problem-solving not problem avoidant.

Blow your horn.

MIMSISM # 09 SEEK TO UNDERSTAND WHERE EVERY MAN HAS FAILED AND WHERE EVERY MAN HAS WON.

Read autobiographies and biographies; your success is in every turn of the page. The history of individuals and institutions when read will open the new doors to innovative visions and revitalize suppressed thoughts.

MIMSISM # 10 LOCATE THE ENEMY WITHIN YOU AND DEFEAT IT.

Each of us has an internal enemy that must be defeated before success can be viewed and enjoyed. Success without defeating that enemy will only cause you to fight it again and again.

MIMSISM # 11 NEVER MISS THE OPPORTUNITY TO DO INCREDIBILITY HARD THINGS WITH INCREDIBLE SMART PEOPLE.

Blow your horn.

When seeking to go forward choose the hard, broken and rough path to success. Help will appear.

MIMSISM's # 12 DO NOT BE AFRAID TO PLAY YOUR GAME ABOVE THE RIM.

When playing the game of life and it is your turn at bat swing for the fences and beyond, your success is in the parking lots.

MIMSISM # 13 CHANGE IT, FIX IT CREATE IT MOVE IT, IMPROVE-IT, CHALLENGE IT, CONTROL IT, OWN IT AND LOVE IT.

If success is what you request do all these things.

MIMSISM # 14 UNDERSTAND THE WHO, THE WHAT, THE WHEN, THE HOW, THE WHY

Blow your horn.

AND THE WHEREOF INFORMATION THAT IS PRESENTED BEFORE YOU.

MIMSISM # 15 THE BEST WAY TO GET ON YOUR FEET IS TO GET OFF YOUR ASS.

As a young man, my grandfather Ervin E. Larvan would tell me "Laziness will kill you and success comes to no one that sleeps".

MIMSISM # 16 BEING WEALTHY IN MANY WAY IN AMERICA IS EASY; BEING UNDERPRIVILEGED IS HARD, BOTH REQUIRE WORK AND DEDICATION YOU MAKE THE CHOOSE.

MIMSISM # 17 NEVER LET YOUR THINKING OR OTHERS THINKING DROWN OR RESTRICTIONS YOUR ACCOMPLISHMENT.

Blow your horn.

On average every person has 3 to 5 good ideas a day. To turn a good into a great day just act upon 3 of those ideas.

MIMSISM # 18 NEVER GIVE UP

The ability to complete the task is an embedded skill. Your internal drives and the need to finish any task is the foundation of success. Never give up on anyone, anybody or any task.

MIMSISM # 19 VOLUNTEERING IS A POOR PERSON'S VEHICLE TO ACCOMPLISHMENT AND RECOGNITION.

When you give your time and expect nothing in return, and success will find you when you least expect it.

 Blow your horn.

MIMSISM # 20 BUSINESSES IS AN ART, NOT A SCIENCE KNOWS THE DIFFERENCE BETWEEN THE TWO BEFORE YOU OCCUPY YOURSELF.

MIMSISM # 21 BUSINESSES IS ACHIEVED WITH BOTH YOUR HANDS IN FRONT OF YOU. BUT OBSERVE OF THE HANDS OF YOUR COMPETITORS.

There are others that will not have the same ethics and principles that you respect.

MIMSISM # 22. THINK HUGE ABOUT ALL THINGS. SMALL THINKERS ROB CORNERS STORES.

Your thoughts drive your actions and your directions. The larger you aspire to be the greater the reward and the success.

Blow your horn.

MIMSISM # 23 BE AN EARLY ADOPTER AND A QUICK RELEASE.

Locate the trends and patterns in everything around you. Understand them to integrate and advance them. Success,

MIMSISM # 24 EVERYDAY AT 6:30 PM, ASSESS HOW FAR YOU HAVE KICKED THE CAN.

A daily self-evaluation is a great way to governor your time and tracks your actions to match them to your goals.

MIMSISM # 25 EVERYTHING HAS VALUE; WHAT IS YOUR WORTH? WHAT DO YOU BRING TO THE TABLE EACH DAY?

To understand your true value is ESSENTIAL in making decisions and that will affect you in

Blow your horn.

the future. Remember your value must modify daily to be worth your salt.

MIMSISM # 26 DRIVE YOUR COMMERCE WITH BALANCE AND CONVICTION.

Everyone has their own personal commerce (an interchange of goods or commodities) to be sold. It is your job to its control and does it with confidence.

MIMSISM # 27 IF YOU ARE NOT MOVING FORWARD, THEN YOUR MEANS OF TRANSPORTATION IS IN REVERSE.

The only way to move forward is with someone, check your passengers if you are not moving in the right direction.

MIMSISM # 28 LIFE WILL HAVE ITS UPS AND ITS DOWNS, MAKE SURE YOU ARE UNPREJUDICED.

Blow your horn.

Without preconception; unbiased; impartial an up or a down has no lasting effect on you.

MIMSISM # 29 WHEN YOU THINK YOU HAVE DONE ENOUGH, DO MORE and MORE.

MIMSISM # 30 THE THINKS THAT MAKES YOU ANGER IS THE WINNER AND YOU LOSE EVERY TIME.

Never give in to your anger, control it, and repress it for a better good.

Blow your horn.

Quotes Un-Defined

Blow your horn.

MIMSISM # 40 IT IS WHAT YOU DO IN YOUR COMMUNITY THAT MATTERS LONG AFTER YOU HAVE MOVED.

MIMSISM# 41 WHEN YOUR EYES BECOME OPEN YOU'RE ACCURATE VISION IS REVIVED.

MIMSISM # 43 MAKE A DECISION

MIMSISM # 44 RESPECT SHOULD BE EXTENDS TO ANYONE YOU MAY ENCOUNTER.

Blow your horn.

MIMSISM # 45 DEMAND EXCELLENCE AND BE WILLING TO PAY FOR IT.

MIMSISM # 46 CHOOSE EMPLOYMENT THAT CHALLENGES YOU IN EVERY ASPECT OF LIFE.

MIMSISM # 48 WHEN A DECISION, CHOICE OR JUDGMENT MUST BE MADE DO 3 THINGS... FIRST, GATHER ALL THE DETAILS, SECOND, CANDIDLY DISCUSS THEM WITH SOMEONE, THIRD, SLEEP OR NAP ON IT...THERE IS CLARITY AFTER SLUMBER.

MIMSISM # 49 TAKE FULL RESPONSIBILITY FOR YOUR ACTIONS AND THE OUTCOME.

Blow your horn.

MIMSISM # 53 I WANT TO EARN THE RIGHT TO DETEST PRESIDENT BARACK OBAMA…I WANT TO TAKE HOME MORE THAN $250,000 A YEAR.

MIMSISM # 54 THE WORD SELAH MEANS TO REFLEX AND UNDERSTAND WHAT IT MEANS AND SEEK TO COMPREHEND THE SUPERIOR GOOD OF ALL. (THIS WORD APPEARS IN THE BOOK OF PSALMS 71 TIMES).

MIMSISM # 60 WHEN SEEKING TO MOVE FORWARD OR UPWARD IN ANY SITUATION REMEMBER TO INSULATE YOU, BUT TAKE CARE NOT TO ISOLATE.

MIMSISM # 61 A MAN WITH VALUE TRUMPS A SUCCESSFUL MAN ANYDAY.

Blow your horn.

MIMSISM # 63 WHAT DOES NOT FIT A NEED FOR TODAY MAY BECOME A GOLD INDIGO OF TOMORROW.

MIMSISM # 64 THE MORE YOU FAMILIARIZE YOURSELF WITH THE CHANGES IN LIFE BE THEY ESOTERIC OR CEREBRAL, THE GREATER THE REWARDS YOU WILL TAKE DELIVERY OF AND RECEIVE A COMPLETE AND BALANCE LIFE.

MIMSISM # 71 THE HUMAN MIND IS NOT A POOL THAT NEEDS FILLING TO BE USED, BUT IS CHARCOAL THAT NEEDS IGNITING.

MIMSISM # 72 WHEN IT COMES TO ACCEPTED WISDOM, IT IS MOST EFFICIENT

Blow your horn.

AND RELIABLE TO THINK IN MONUMENTAL DEEDS THAN IMAGING IN ECONOMY SCALE.

MIMSISM #76 WHAT YOU KNOW, BUY IT. WHAT YOU DON'T KNOW, LEARN IT. WHAT YOU NEED TO KNOW, SEEK IT.

MIMSISM # 78 IF YOU WANT TO GO FAST GO ALONE IF YOU WANT TO GO FAR GO TOGETHER.

MIMSISM # 79 ONE'S ATTITUDE CREATES SPACE FOR NEW GROWTH AND NEW POSSIBILITIES.

MIMSISM # 80A IF ONE DOES NOT HAVE; IT IS BECAUSE ONE DOES NOT ASK.

Blow your horn.

MIMSISM # 82 ALWAYS DO THE RIGHT THING EVEN IF THE RIGHT THING IS THE HARDEST THING.

MIMSISM # 82A NEVER ACQUIRES MONEY YOU HAVE NOT PAID FOR.

MIMSISM # 83 IF YOU WANT TO GROW YOUR ENTERPRISE YOU MUST ATTACK ON ALL FRONTS WITH ALL FORCES.

MIMSISM # 84 XEROX COPIES DOCUMENTS··· YOU ARE AN ORIGINAL, ONLY MADE IN GODS IMAGE.

Blow your horn.

MIMSISM # 85 THE PURSUIT OF MONEY MERELY, IS A MONOTONOUS JOURNAL TO SPACES AND PLACES THAT LACK GROWTH AND REAL QUALITY OF LIFE.

MIMSISM # 91 BE READY TO LOSE MORE THAN YOU WIN. LEARNING HAS A REAL COST AND A GENUINE RECOMPENSE.

MIMSISM # 92 TIMES IS THE ONLY THING YOU CANNOT GET MORE OF, USE IT INTELLIGENTLY.

MIMSISM # 93 LEARN TO EAT YOUR OWN DOG FOOD.

Blow your horn.

MIMSISM # 94 YOU MUST DO INCREDIBLE THINGS…LIFE WILL NOT PRESENT YOU A GOLD MEDAL FOR DOING NOTHING.

MIMSISM # 95 NEVER GET YOUR BREAD FROM SOMEONE LED BY OF QUESTIONABLE CHARACTER.

MIMSISM # 96 ARRIVE AT WORK ONE HOUR EARLY AND STAY PASS QUITTING TIME.

MIMSISM # 97 JUDGE YOUR PERSONAL SUCCESS BY WHAT YOU HAD TO GIVE UP IN ORDER TO GET IT.

MIMSISM # 97A YOU MUST DO INCREDIBLE THINGS…LIFE WILL NOT PRESENT YOU A

Blow your horn.

GOLD MEDAL FOR DOING NOTHING. (SEE MIMSISM # 29)

MIMSISM # 98 TIME IS THE ONLY THING YOU CANNOT GET MORE OF, USE IT INTELLIGENTLY.

MIMSISM # 100 EVERY LIFE HAS BEEN PREARRANGED WITH THREE (3) OPPORTUNITIES TO BECOME VICTORIOUS AND SUCCESSFUL, HAS YOUR APERTURE BEEN BREACHED?

MIMSISM # 101 FEARS SHOULD BE YOUR GREATEST MOTIVATOR, EMBRACE IT AND MAKE IT WORK FOR YOU.

Blow your horn.

MIMSISM #102 SLEEP IS THE MOTHERS MILK FOR THE ENHANCEMENT OF EVERY SKILL YOU WHICH TO MASTER.

MIMSISM # 103 DID YOU ATTEND COLLEGE/UNIVERSITY TO GET AN EDUCATION OR TO GET A JOB?

MIMSISM # 104 NEVER TAKE ANY MONEY YOU DID NOT WORK FOR.

MIMSISM # 105 BREAKING THESE RULES WILL OPEN NEW DOOR AND A FEW STAINGLASS WINDOWS.

MIMSISM # 106 EVERYONE IS A MILLIONAIRE. IT IS HOW YOU USE THE

Blow your horn.

TOOLS AND ASSETS AROUND YOU THAT MAKE THOSE MILLIONS VISIBLE.

MIMSISM # 107 IF CHANGE IS WHAT YOU SEEK IN LIFE- JUST BREAK THE RULES.

MIMSMIS # 108 DON'T WORRY ABOUT IT – DO SOMETHING ABOUT IT – IF YOU CAN'T DO SOMETHING ABOUT IT – DON'T WORRY ABOUT IT. WORRYING HAS NEVER SOLVED A PREDICAMENT.

MIMSISM # 109 WHEN MAKING A DECISION ALLOW A GOODNIGHT SLEEP TO PRESEED. THERE IS CLARITY AND NEW VISION IN THE DARKNESS.

Blow your horn.

MIMSISM # 110 NEVER END A DAY WITHOUT SPEAKING A WORD OF ENDEARMENT.

MIMSISM # 111 NEVER LIE OR MISLEAD ANYONE. IF IT IS A FRIEND YOU DESTROY THE RELATIONSHIP. IF IT IS YOUR ENERGY – WHY LIE TO THEM?

MIMSISM # 112 LIFE WILL PRESENT YOU WITH THREE TO FIVE OPPORTUNITIES TO BE SUCCESSFUL. MAKE SURE YOU ARE PREPARED.

MIMSISM # 113 TO GO FAR AND LAST LONGER INVOLVE THE CORRECT PEOPLE IN YOUR MISSION BY GIVING THEM YOUR VISION.

Blow your horn.

MIMSISM # 114 THE FIRST RULE OF COMMUNICATING "<u>EVERY QUESTION OR STATEMENT DOES NOT REQUIRE AN IMMEDIATE RESPONSE</u>" DELAYING YOUR RESPONSE INDICATES A STROKE OF GENIUS ON YOUR PART.

MIMSISM # 115 WHEN FACED WITH A DILEMMA THE SAFE AND TRUSTED SOLUTION IS NOT ALWAYS THE EASY SOLUTION TO SWALLOW.

MIMSISM # 116 GREAT JAZZ OPENS THE EYES, CLEARS THE LUNGS AND STIMULATES GREAT BLOOD FLOW.

Blow your horn.

MIMSISM # 117 WELL DRESS FOOD, WINE, AND PEOPLE ARE IMPORTANT IN YOUR DAYS. THEY ADD SEASONING TO YOUR IMAGININGS AND MODE.

MIMSISM # 118 WHEN YOU MAKE A MISTAKE THERE ARE THREE ACTIONS YOU MUST PROFORM, <u>APOLOGIES,</u> <u>ATONE</u> FOR IT, & <u>AVERT</u> IT FROM HAPPENING AGAIN.

MIMSISM # 119 EVERY WORKING SECOND MUST BE WOKE.

MIMSISM # 120 YESTERDAY WAS DESIGNED FOR <u>REGRETS,</u> TODAY IS DESIGN FOR <u>ACCOMPLISHMENT</u> AND TOMORROW DESIGN FOR YOUR <u>IMAGINING</u> NEVER TRY SUBSTITUTING ONE FOR ANOTHER.

Blow your horn.

MIMSISM # 121 WHEN CHOSEN A MATE PICK SOMEONE THAT LIKES YOU NOT THE PERSON YOU LIKE.

MIMSISM # 122 NEVER SPEAK IN CONCLUSIONS UNLESS YOU HAVE COMPLETED YOUR GOALS.

Blow your horn.

OVER AND DONE WITH

NOT YET

Blow your horn.

Blow your horn.

Blow your horn.

"ACHIEVEMENT"

Successes are many in life and they come in all shapes, forms, and sizes. Everyone is successful. To be successful requires applying various forms of disciplines, decrees, and new rules. The early in existence you adapt your standard of living to these do's and do not's with some modifications when needed. The earlier success will become a central part of your

Blow your horn.

day to day life. The key to being a successful per is to recognize when you have received success in life. There is no such thing as a small success there are only successes. Here are some successes that you may not have recognized: when you have a TRUE friend, purchase of any item needed, a clear thought, a word that brings you joy, more money earned, defeating fears, solving a problem of any size, recovering a dream losing a

Blow your horn.

battle but winning the war, thinking before you speak, undercover new you and many more. Invest in successes. Meaning put your time and money into those things that achieve success in others not in yourself.

Blow your horn.

Blow your horn.

KEYWORDS AND PHRASES THAT DRIVE SUCCESSES

Directions, Leadership, Clarity, Understanding, and Values

 Blow your horn.

www.ingramcontent.com/pod-product-compliance
Lightning Source LLC
Chambersburg PA
CBHW040240220526
45473CB00001B/315